WORKBOOK

LEVEL B

A Hen in a Fox's Den

by Donald Rasmussen and Lynn Goldberg

BASIC READING
BERKELEY·CALIFORNIA

To Parents and Teachers

Donald Rasmussen and Lynn Goldberg developed the BASIC READING SERIES (BRS) in the early 1960s at the Miquon School, a small parent-teacher cooperative near Philadelphia. At that time, most children were taught to read using the "sight" or "look-say" method epitomized by the "Dick and Jane" readers, and many were left behind. Don and Lynn knew there must be a better way, so they spent five years developing their own reading program based on the work of the renowned linguist Leonard Bloomfield. They called their method *"inductive whole-word phonics, with a strong linguistics research base."*

After tryouts in inner-city and suburban schools around the country and almost a dozen revisions, the BASIC READING SERIES was published by Science Research Associates (SRA) and enjoyed great success. Over the years, other reading methods have come and then gone out of favor. Now, decades later, phonics is recognized as the scientific approach to reading instruction, and the BASIC READING SERIES is once again available.

BRS is divided into six levels — Levels A to F — with a reader and a workbook for each level. In Level B, children are introduced to three new vowel sound-spelling relationships: *e* as in *pet*, *o* as in *pot*, and *u* as in *cut*. The new words introduced follow the same pattern as the words in Level A: 3-letter words in which a vowel appears between two consonants. In addition, children meet initial *g* and *y*, final *x*, and six new 14 exceptional words that do not belong to a sound-spelling pattern.

The BRS Workbooks

The workbooks for BRS contain material with which children can practice their decoding skills independently of teacher direction. The decoding experiences thus provided increase the children's opportunities to discover sound-spelling relationships and to develop automatic word recognition. The workbooks are also an aid to vocabulary, word-meaning, and concept development, as they lead children to associate words with appropriate visual images and challenge children to deal with the meanings of words, phrases, and sentences. Finally, the workbooks are a useful tool with which to evaluate the children's decoding progress.

The workbook for Level B has six sections of exercises, which correspond (in their sound-spelling patterns only) to the six sections of the Level B reader, *A Hen in a Fox's Den*. The exercises are not tied to the story content of the reader, however. Each section is identified by numbered tabs in the margins of its pages and begins with a word chart that reviews familiar words from Level A and presents new words for that section of Level B. Each section progresses from simple exercises based on single words and phrases to more complex exercises involving phrases and sentences.

The workbook is easy to use. Children answer each item in one of three ways: by circling a word or phrase; by writing a numeral in a box; or by placing an X in a circle. Since no handwriting skill is needed, the children's reading progress is kept independent of their handwriting progress. The reading lesson can proceed regardless of the children's handwriting abilities.

Some suggestions for the most effective use of the Level B workbook:

1. Do not ask the children to do the work in a given section of the workbook until they have become acquainted with the sound-spelling patterns in that section. You may want to begin each section of the workbook by reading the word charts for that section with the children. Have the children read up and down the columns, and discuss any unfamiliar words with them before proceeding to the exercises.

2. Throughout the first section of Level B, take care to see that each child understands the directions and is following them correctly before encouraging them to proceed on their own.

3. If a child does not recognize a pictured object, simply tell them what it is.

4. Whenever possible, correct the children's work with them, reading the words, phrases, and sentences aloud and discussing the pictures. The more the children *hear* the words while looking at them, the greater will be their chance to develop automatic word recognition.

5. Try to assess the reasons for the children's errors and deal with them appropriately. Sometimes, as on the riddle pages, an error may be caused by faulty reasoning rather than by faulty decoding. At this stage, accurate decoding is a more important goal than perfect reasoning, and a child who decodes correctly but reasons poorly should still be praised for their reading.

6. Note that the "Can it?" exercises are purposely written without clear-cut answers to every item. These pages should be discussed but not corrected. Make it a general rule *for all formats* not to put undue stress on getting the right answer. Instead, put the stress on accurate decoding and the enjoyment of using reading skills in a problem-solving situation.

Email all inquiries to:
Peter Rasmussen, Editor
info@BasicReading.com

Website: BasicReading.com
ISBN 978-1-937547-02-8

_ a _	_ i _	_ e _	_ o _	_ u _
bat	bit	bet		but
cat			cot	cut
			dot	
		get	got	
hat	hit		hot	hut
		jet	jot	jut
	kit			
	lit	let	lot	
mat		met		
Nat		net	not	nut
pat	pit	pet	pot	
rat			rot	rut
sat	sit	set		
		wet		
		yet		

1

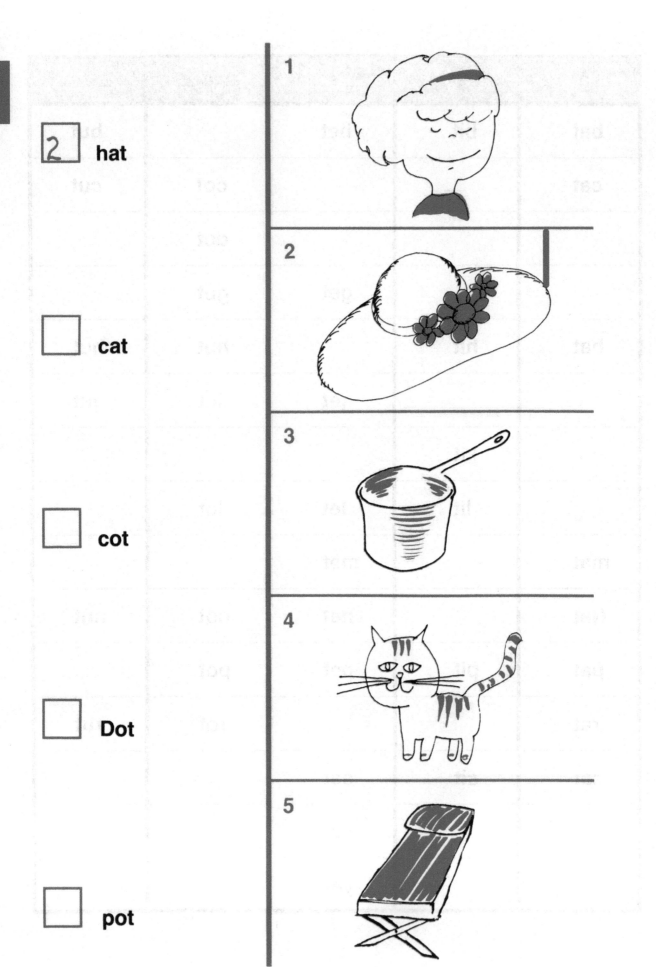

2	hat
	cat
	cot
	Dot
	pot

2

☐ jet

☐ net

☐ pet

☐ hut

☐ nut

get

(jet)

jot

pot

got

dot

yet

pot

pet

hut

not

nut

hat

hot

hit

hit

hut

hat

wet

yet

met

dot

cot

cat

met

not

net

cut

cot

cat

dot

pot

pat

met

net

mat

1

 A pot tips.

 A cot tips.

 The pets met.

 The pigs met.

○ Dan cuts.

○ Dot cuts.

 A pet is wet.

 A net is wet.

3	The van got into a rut.
	The pets got wet.
	The pot is hot.
	The pet is in the net.

The pig began to get — yet. / (wet.) / set.

The cat met a big — pot. / pit. / pet.

The cab is in a bad — hut. / nut. / rut.

The pets sat in a — pat. / pit. / pot.

⊗ Tim said, "The pet has a lot of nuts."

◯ Jim said, "The pet has a lot of nets."

◯ "Rags did not get it yet," said Al.

◯ "I let Rags get the net," said Al.

◯ "Tim's pet is in the pot," said Dot.

◯ "Dan's pot is in the pit," said Dot.

◯ "I did not let Dot into the hut," said Rags.

◯ "I did not let Kit into the hut," said Rags.

☐ "I got it in a net," said Kim,
"but I got wet."

☐ "It is hot," said Tim,
"but the cot is not hot yet."

☐ "The bad pet hid," said Tim,
"but I can get him."

☐ "I can pet it," said Pam,
"and I can get it wet."

Dot can get into the —— net.
jet.
pet.

Al met Peg at the —— hut.
hat.
hit.

Wag let Kit into his —— pot.
pet.
pit.

Dot cuts the big —— net.
not.
nut.

Can it?

○ Can a net rip?

○ Can a nut fit in a net?

○ Can a pet get hot?

○ Can a pot get wet?

○ Can a dot pet a pot?

○ Can Dot cut a nut?

○ Can a hut sit in a pot?

○ Can a pet get a lot of nuts?

It can get hot.

It can get wet.

It is as big as a hat.

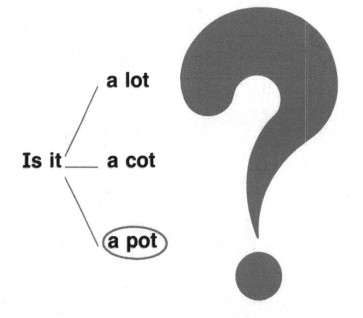

Is it ____
- a lot
- a cot
- (a pot)

It can sit in a hut.

It can get a lot of nuts.

It can get big and fat.

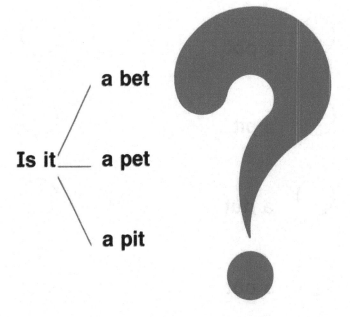

Is it ____
- a bet
- a pet
- a pit

Is it in the hut?

⊗ **a bag**

○ **a dot**

○ **a pot**

○ **a rut**

○ **a pit**

○ **a jet**

○ **a nut**

○ **a net**

○ **a cot**

○ **a pet**

14

It can get a rip in it.

A pet can get in it.

It is as big as a pot.

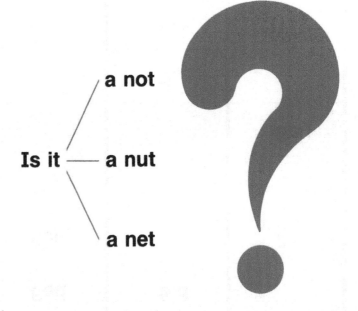

Is it ── a not

a nut

a net

A van can get into it.

A cab can get into it.

Wag and Kit can sit in it.

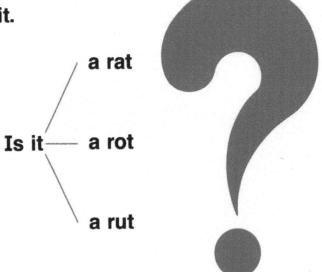

Is it ── a rat

a rot

a rut

_ a _	_ i _	_ e _	_ o _	_ u _
bag	big	beg		bug
	dig		dog	dug
	fig		fog	
hag			hog	hug
	jig		jog	jug
lag		leg	log	lug
	pig	peg		
rag				rug
tag				tug
wag	wig			

☐ dog

☐ hog

☐ log

☐ jug

☐ rug

1

2

3

4

5

2

☐ **leg**

☐ **Peg**

☐ **beg**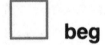

☐ **bug**

☐ **dug**

⊗ a big dog
◯ a big log

◯ a fat bug
◯ a fat bag

◯ a big map
◯ a hot mug

◯ a pet pig
◯ a wet fog

◯ a wet rut
◯ a wet rug

◯ a sad dog
◯ a mad hog

2

○ **a dog in the fog**

○ **a hog in the hut**

○ **jets in the fog**

○ **pets and a rug**

○ **a hog in a jug**

○ **a bug in a rug**

○ **a bug and a nut**

○ **a jug and a mug**

○ **a pet in the fog**

○ **a dog in the log**

○ **a dog and a log**

○ **a bug and a leg**

○ Jim has a bad leg.

○ Jim sat to cut logs.

○ Meg can hug the pets.

○ Meg can lug the pots.

○ A fat bug bit Wag's leg.

○ A big dog dug a pit.

○ The hog sits.

○ The dog naps.

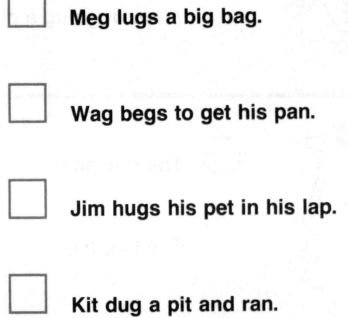

☐ Meg lugs a big bag.

☐ Wag begs to get his pan.

☐ Jim hugs his pet in his lap.

☐ Kit dug a pit and ran.

Kim can hit it. It is a

- pot.
- peg.
- pet.

It is in a hut. It is a

- rut.
- rug.
- rat.

The man can cut it. It is a

- log.
- fog.
- leg.

Dot has a pal. It is

- Peg.
- a pet.
- a pot.

2

◯ Kim said to Wag, "Sit and beg."

◯ Tim said to Rags, "Sit and dig."

◯ "The dog dug in the rug," said Dad.

◯ "I dug a pit in the fog," said the hog.

◯ "I can tug at the rug," said the hog.

◯ "I can get into the jug," said the bug.

◯ Jim said, "I can hug the dog."

◯ The dog said, "I can tug at the rug."

☐ Dad said, "It is big. Peg can hug it, but Peg cannot lug it."

☐ Dad said, "It's a bad bug. It bit the dog's leg."

☐ The cat said, "I can lug Kit. I can get Kit to the rug."

☐ The dog said, "I can tag Kit. Kit's leg is in the rug."

Tim is not sad. Tim hugs his —— dog.
—— hog.
—— Dad.

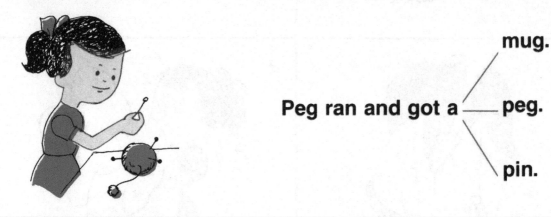

Peg ran and got a —— mug.
—— peg.
—— pin.

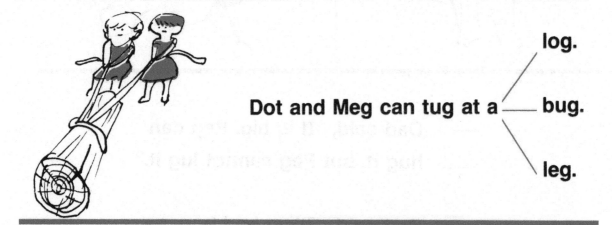

Dot and Meg can tug at a —— log.
—— bug.
—— leg.

Tim's pet began to tug at his —— let.
—— leg.
—— log.

Can it?

○ Can a rug fit in a hut?

○ Can a jug get hot and wet?

○ Can a bug hug a leg?

○ Can a bug lug a log?

○ Can a hog jig in the fog?

○ Can a dog dig in the fog?

○ Can Peg fit in a pot?

○ Can Peg tug at a rug?

2

It is Meg's pet.

It can nap in a hut.

It can dig a big pit.

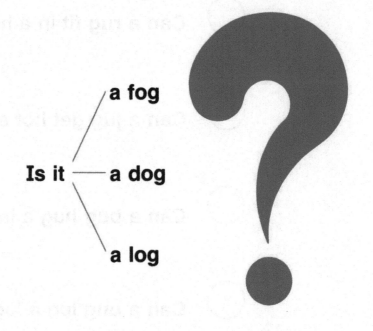

Is it — a fog / a dog / a log

It is tin.

It can tip.

It can get hot and wet.

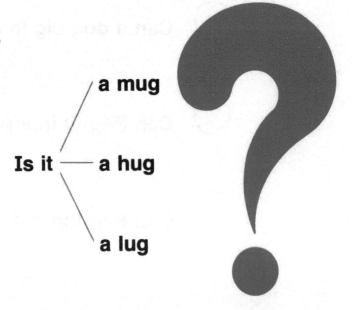

Is it — a mug / a hug / a lug

Is it in the fog?

○ a cab   ○ a van

○ a dog   ○ a log

○ a rug   ○ the ruts

○ Meg   ○ Peg

○ a hat   ○ a hog

It is a big, big mat.

It fits in a hut.

Dot can tug at it.

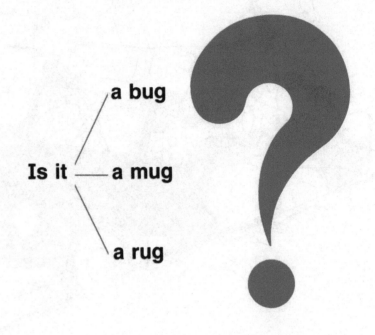

Is it —— a bug / a mug / a rug

I can lug a big bag.

I can tug at a big rug.

I can hug lots of pets.

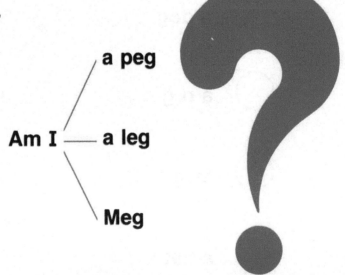

Am I —— a peg / a leg / Meg

_ a _	_ i _	_ e _	_ o _	_ u _
	bin	Ben		bun
Dan		den	Don	
fan	fin			fun
				gun
		hen		
		Ken		
man		men		
pan	pin	pen		
ran				run
				sun
tan	tin	ten		
an	in		on	

☐ hen

☐ den

☐ pen

☐ men

☐ ten

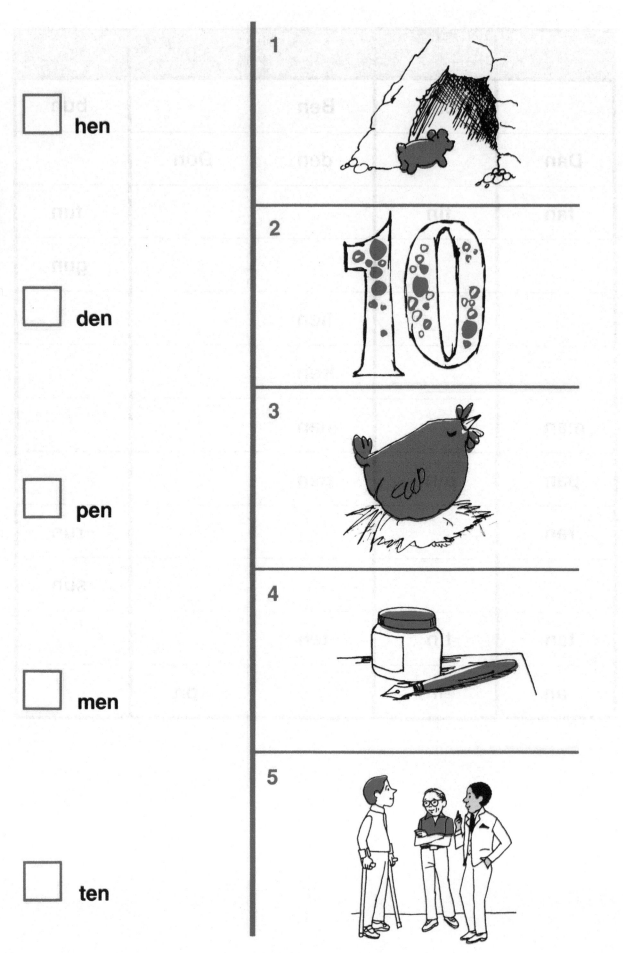

1

2

3

4

5

☐ sun	**1**
☐ bun	**2**
☐ Ben	**3**
☐ run	**4**
☐ rug	**5**

him

hen

ham

mat

Meg

men

pan

pen

pin

ban

bin

bun

Dan

den

Don

run

rut

rug

○ **Meg's bun**

○ **Meg's bug**

○ **Ben's pen**

○ **Ben's pet**

○ **Dot's nut**

○ **Dad's net**

○ **Dad's mug**

○ **Sam's rug**

○ **Dan's pen**

○ **Dad's den**

○ **a hen's hut**

○ **a hen's pan**

○ Ben's hens run into the pen.

○ Ben lets the hen sit by the pan.

○ Don has ten big buns.

○ Don has ten tin men.

○ Pam has fun in the hen's pen.

○ Pam met a lot of pigs.

○ Ben gets a pen in Dad's den.

○ Ben sits on a cot in the den.

1

2

3

4

☐ Dad's pen is by the pad.

☐ Meg runs in the sun.

☐ Dot has ham on a bun.

☐ The dog has fun in the pen.

The fat hen runs in the ——

- sun.
- bun.
- fun.

Dad sits on it in his ——

- pen.
- hen.
- den.

It is fun to jog and ——

- run.
- rut.
- rug.

Dot has a pal. It is ——

- Peg.
- a pet.
- a pot.

○ "It's fun to run in the sun," said the hen.

○ "It's lots of fun in the sun," said Meg.

○ "Is the pen in the den?" said Dad.

○ "Is the pin in the bun?" said Dan.

○ Don said, "Rags sits in his pen."

○ Dad said, "Run and get the hens, Ben."

○ Don said, "The men can lug the rug."

○ Don said, "The men had lots of legs."

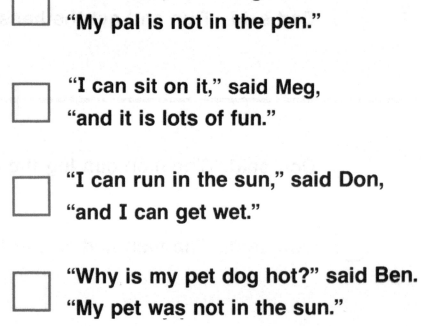

☐ "I am sad," said Big Hen.
"My pal is not in the pen."

☐ "I can sit on it," said Meg,
"and it is lots of fun."

☐ "I can run in the sun," said Don,
"and I can get wet."

☐ "Why is my pet dog hot?" said Ben.
"My pet was not in the sun."

If Ken gets wet, let him sit in the —— sit.

sun.

set.

If Dot digs in the sun, it is —— fun.

fog.

fan.

If the dog sits on a log, it can —— big.

beg.

bug.

If a pet is hot, let it nap on a —— met.

mat.

mug.

Can it?

○ Can ham fit on a bun?

○ Can a hen fit in a den?

○ Can a hen run in a pen?

○ Can a sun set in a den?

○ Can a bun run in the sun?

○ Can ten men get in a jet?

○ Can ten men sit on a pin?

○ Can ten hens get on a cot?

Is it in the pigpen?

○ Don in a hat

○ a hog in a pit

○ a pet in a bag

○ nuts in a jug

○ a hen by Don

○ a bug on a log

○ a pig at a pan

○ a log in a pen

○ Don in the sun

○ men in a cab

3

43

It is big and hot.

Men sit in it and get tan.

It sets, but it cannot sit.

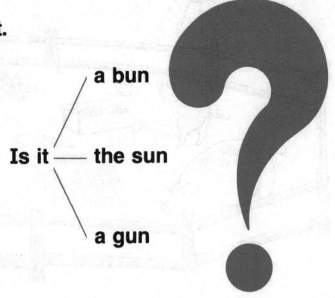

Is it —— a bun

Is it —— the sun

Is it —— a gun

Don is my pal.

I am not his pet.

I am not yet a man.

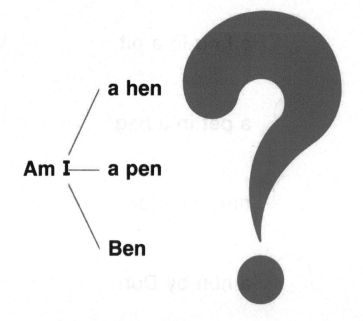

Am I —— a hen

Am I —— a pen

Am I —— Ben

Is it in the sun?

○ The hen sits in the sun and hits the pots.

○ The hen runs to get the fat bugs.

○ Don sits on a big log in the sun.

○ A pet sits on the log.

○ Don has a big, big hat.

○ Pam sits in the sun and has a lot of pots.

○ Pam sits in the sun and sits on a hen.

It can run and dig in the sun.

It can get a lot of bugs.

It has a lot of fun in its pen.

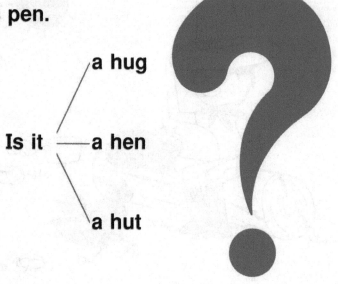

Is it — a hug
a hen
a hut

I had ten tin men.

I had a cap.

My dog Rags is my pal.

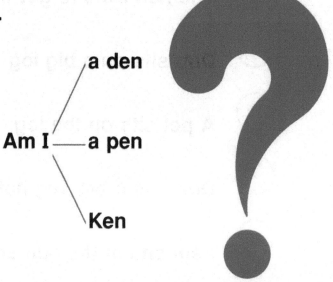

Am I — a den
a pen
Ken

_ a _	_ i _	_ e _	_ o _	_ u _
bad	bid	bed		bud
		fed		
lad	lid	led		
mad				mud
		Ned	nod	
pad			pod	
	rid	red	rod	
		Ted		
cap				cup
	hip		hop	
map			mop	
		pep	pop	pup
tap	tip		top	
				up

☐ bed

4

☐ bud

☐ **mud**

☐ mad

☐ **Ned**

1

2

3

4

5

☐ **cup**

☐ **pup**

☐ **pop**

☐ **mop**

☐ **top**

1

2

3

4

5

cot

cup

cap

top

tap

tot

fig

fed

fog

nod

Ned

Nan

bed

bad

but

pup

pop

pep

- ○ a hen's hop
- ○ Ken's top

- ○ a fat pup
- ○ a big cup

- ○ a wet mop
- ○ a red mat

- ○ a fat bud
- ○ a big bed

- ○ Nan's rod
- ○ a man's nod

- ○ a hen's hop
- ○ a pen's top

○ Ted fed his pup.

○ Ted let his pup sit by him.

4

○ The bug hops on its legs.

○ The bug hops on the rod.

○ The mad hen hid by a log.

○ The log has a bud on it.

○ The pup got mud on its legs.

○ The pup ran on a rug.

☐ The cup is by the pot.

☐ The mop is by the bed.

☐ The bug is on the bud.

☐ The pup is on a rug.

Ted has to mop up the ⎯ mad.

⎯ mud.

⎯ dam.

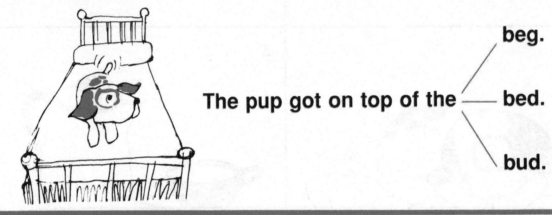

The pup got on top of the ⎯ beg.

⎯ bed.

⎯ bud.

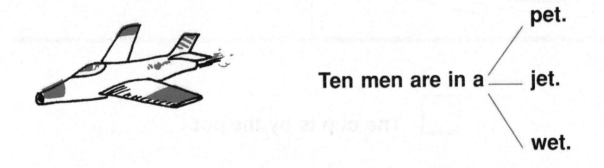

Ten men are in a ⎯ pet.

⎯ jet.

⎯ wet.

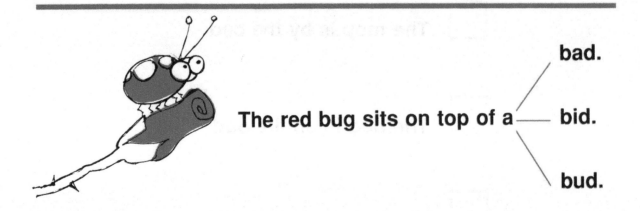

The red bug sits on top of a ⎯ bad.

⎯ bid.

⎯ bud.

○ Ned said, "The mop is on the big bed."

○ Ted said, "The pup is on my bed."

○ Kim said, "Why is the bud in the cup?"

○ Kim said, "Why is the pup in the mud?"

○ "I am not red yet," said the bud.

○ "I am not fed yet," said the pup.

○ "The dog is on top of the bed," said Meg.

○ "My log is on top of the bud," said Meg.

☐ Peg said, "I can hop!
It's fun to hop and hop."

☐ Ted said, "It can pop up.
And it's lots of fun."

☐ Jim said, "Get the mop!
It's wet, and I can mop it up."

☐ Meg sat by the pup and said,
"Hop up on my lap."

If Ned gets mud on the mat, get him a _____

pop.

mop.

map.

If a pup is fed, it gets a lot of _____

pet.

pen.

pep.

If a man sits and nods, get him a _____

bed.

bad.

bid.

The bug is on the _____

fog.

dog.

log.

Can it?

○ Can a pup hop in the mud?

○ Can a nod hop on a pod?

○ Can a mop get rid of mud?

○ Can a big bug hop on a red bud?

○ Can a pup sip pop in a cup?

○ Can a red hen hop in a bed?

○ Can Ted get fed in a bed?

○ Can Ned nod and nap in a bed?

Is it in the mud?

○ a fat pup   ○ sad Peg

○ wet Ned   ○ a bud

○ a red top   ○ a big bed

○ a big cup   ○ wet Meg

○ mad Ted   ○ a wet mop

It is big and fat.

It can jig in lots of mud.

It runs and digs in a pen.

Is it — a fog

a hop

a hog

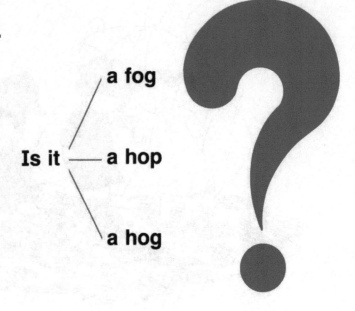

It is Meg's pet.

It is a pal.

It gets up on Meg's bed to nap.

Is it — a cup

a pup

a pop

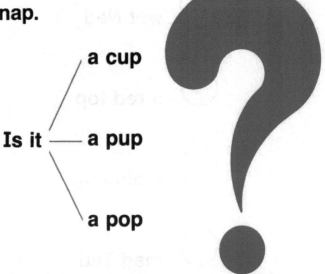

Is it in the Big Top?

○ A dog sits by a man.

○ The dog has a red hat.

○ Ned has a can of pop.

○ A big red hen sits on a pup.

○ A man has lots of pups.

○ The man has a mop.

○ Ten men sit in the mud.

It is Meg's.

It is red.

It cannot hop, but it's lots of fun.

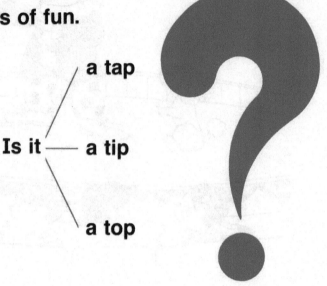

Is it — a tap
Is it — a tip
Is it — a top

It is wet.

A hog can hop in it.

A man can mop it up.

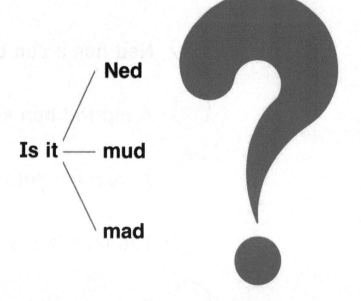

Is it — Ned
Is it — mud
Is it — mad

_ a _	_ i _	_ e _	_ o _	_ u _
				bus
gas				Gus
				us
		yes		
				gum
ham	him	hem		hum
			mom	
Sam				sum
tam	Tim		Tom	
	bib		Bob	
cab			cob	cub
jab			job	
	rib		rob	rub
			sob	
tab				tub
		web		

5

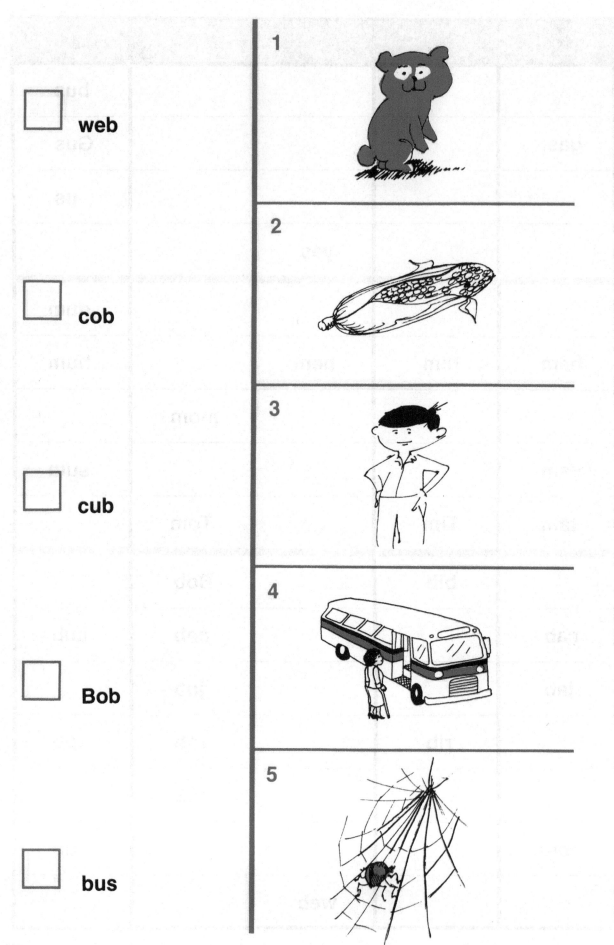

□ web

□ cob

□ cub

□ Bob

□ bus

5

1

2

3

4

5

□ **Mom**

□ **Tom**

□ **gum**

□ **gas**

□ **hum**

1

2

3

4

5

5

mop

Mom

men

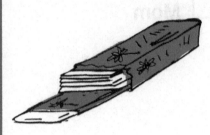

gas

gum

got

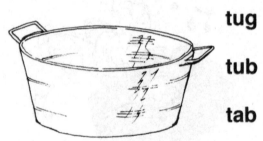

tug

tub

tab

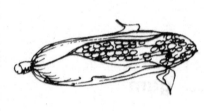

cob

cub

cap

hum

hem

him

bud

bus

Bob

○ **Mom hems.**

○ **Tom hums.**

○ **A pup digs.**

○ **A cup dips.**

○ **A bug runs.**

○ **A pup rubs.**

○ **A pet hugs.**

○ **A bug hums.**

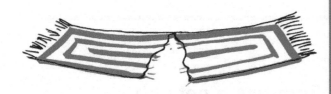

○ **A rug rips.**

○ **A man mops.**

○ **A hen hops.**

○ **A cat hems.**

5

○ The bus gets gas.

○ The bug is on Sis.

○ Tom hugs a cub.

○ Tim runs a cab.

○ Mom fed the ham to Wag.

○ Bob said, "I can hum."

○ Tom has a pet cub.

○ Mom has a tin tub.

☐ Meg led Tom into the bus.

☐ The cub gets wet in the tub.

☐ Tom upsets the tub of suds.

☐ The bug hops into the web.

Val's job is to run a —— cob.

cab.

cup.

Kim did not get on the —— bus.

bug.

bud.

Bob had to tug the cub into the —— ten.

top.

tub.

Peg's hat had a rip, and Peg began to —— rob.

sob.

hum.

○ Min has ten hens and a cub.

○ Ron had a job on the bus.

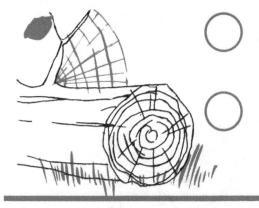

○ The log has a cobweb on it.

○ The tub has a bobcat in it.

5

○ The bug began to rub mud on its leg.

○ The pup sits up in the mud to beg.

○ The bug hums and hops.

○ The dog sits and sobs.

5

1

2

3

4

"If my pup sits in my lap," said Dot,
"I can pet it and hug it."

Tom is in bed and so is Ben.
"Why not hum a bit?" said Mom.

Sam said, "It's fun to sit in the sun.
But my job is to run a bus."

"Let's go on a bus," said Liz.
"Ten of us cannot fit in a cab."

Liz can pin up the
- hum.
- him.
- hem.

Liz ran to get the
- cob.
- cub.
- cab.

Meg got rid of the
- bus.
- buds.
- bugs.

Tom's job is to rub the
- cub.
- tub.
- mud.

5

73

○ Ron said, "Get on the bus, Wag."

○ Don said, "Sit on the bug, Bud."

○ "The sunset is so red," said Roz.

○ "A bug's in the cobweb," said Mom.

○ "The cob is on the top," said Meg.

○ "The cub is in the tub," said Peg.

○ Dot and Ted said, "Run to us, Wag."

○ Mom and Ned said, "Run to the bus, Wag."

Can it?

◯ Can a wet cub run on gas?

◯ Can a fat bug hum by a red bud?

◯ Can a fat cub jab a big rib?

◯ Can a tan cab jab a big bus?

◯ Can a red bib fit in a tin tub?

◯ Can a tan bug hum and sit in a web?

◯ Can a red bug sit and hem a bib?

◯ Can Tom's mom rub a wet bus?

5

Dot can sit in it.

Dot gets wet in it.

Mom rubs suds on Dot in it.

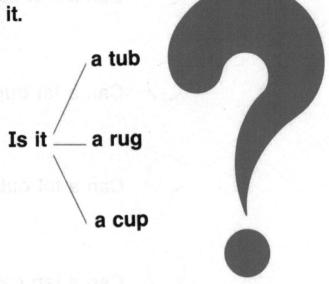

Is it — a tub / a rug / a cup

It can get on Sis.

It can hum and hum.

It can get into a web.

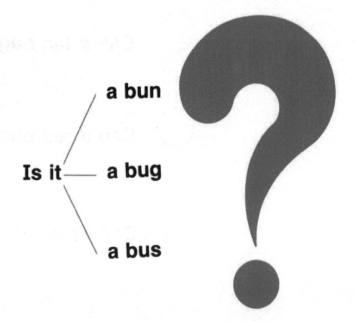

Is it — a bun / a bug / a bus

Is it on the rug?

○ a cub in the tub   ○ a red bug in a web

○ suds in the tub   ○ a red cab in the fog

○ Tom in a hat   ○ suds on the red rug

○ Tim's job is to sob.   ○ a big cup of suds

○ Tom's job is to rub a cub.   ○ Tom hums to the cub.

5

It can go "pop!"

It is lots of fun.

Tom had it and said, "Yum, yum."

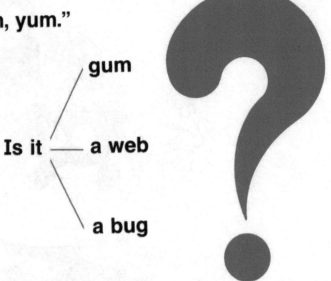

Is it —
- gum
- a web
- a bug

It runs on gas.

A lot of men can get in it.

Roz and Dot can sit in it.

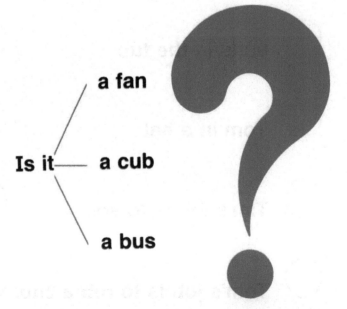

Is it —
- a fan
- a cub
- a bus

_ a _	_ i _	_ e _	_ o _	_ u _
			box	
	fix		fox	
Max	mix			
	six			
wax				
ax			ox	

6

□ ax

□ ox

□ fox

□ box

□ sob

1

2

3

4

5

□ six

□ fix

□ mix

□ Max

□ wax

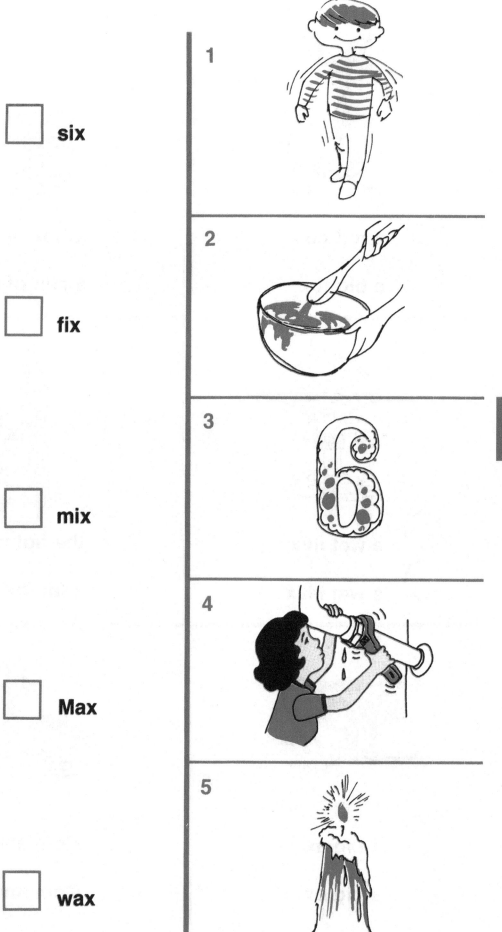

○ a red box

○ a big fox

○ a box of mix

○ a can of wax

○ a wet mix

○ a wet Max

○ the hot wax

○ a fat fox

○ a big ax

○ a big ox

○ Mom and Max

○ Mom and mix

- ◯ **Max and the fox**
- ◯ **mix in a box**

- ◯ **an ax in a log**
- ◯ **an ox on a leg**

- ◯ **six and ten**
- ◯ **six cans of tin**

- ◯ **box in a pen**
- ◯ **fox in a den**

- ◯ **tag on a box**
- ◯ **tap on a fox**

- ◯ **six cups by Sis**
- ◯ **six caps by Max**

○ A red rox runs into his den.

○ A cub is in the big box.

○ Six men led the big ox into a pen.

○ Six bugs ran into the cobweb.

○ Tom can wax the jug.

○ Tom can mix the jam.

○ Roz is six and gets a hat.

○ Roz can fix up the ten men.

Meg's job is to fix the bed.

Jim's job is to rub the jugs and mugs.

Dot's job is to fix the box.

Tom's job is to rub the cub.

The ox can jig on a

- bat.
- box.
- fox.

Mom can fix Jim's

- box.
- wax.
- bus.

Tom can hug a

- cap.
- cab.
- cub.

Pam fed the six

- dogs.
- hogs.
- hens.

6

○ "I can get the fox," said Max.

○ "I can fix the box," said Max.

○ "I can wax it," said Max.

○ "I am six," said Max.

6

○ "Yes, I can fix it," said Mom.

○ "No, I cannot mix it," said Mom.

○ Dad said, "The ax is in the box."

○ Dad said, "The wax is in the can."

1

2

3

6

4

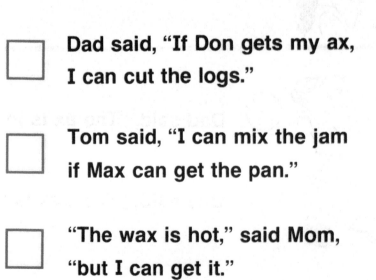

☐ "If the fox cannot fit in the box," said Max, "let it run in the pen."

☐ Dad said, "If Don gets my ax, I can cut the logs."

☐ Tom said, "I can mix the jam if Max can get the pan."

☐ "The wax is hot," said Mom, "but I can get it."

88

Dot's job is to fix a
- box.
- fox.
- ox.

Sam's job is to run a big
- bug.
- box.
- bus.

Wag zips by on the
- web.
- wet.
- wax.

The fan is by the
- fix.
- fox.
- fit.

6

Can it?

◯ Can a red fox sit in a den?

◯ Can Max's ax fit in a box?

◯ Can six cubs mix the wax?

◯ Can six cobs fix the top?

◯ Can a tan ox lug a big box?

◯ Can Mom's pet fox wax a bus?

◯ Can Max rub and wax six jugs?

◯ Can a fox rub suds on an ox in a tub?

6

Is it in the fox's den?

- ⭕ a fat hen
- ⭕ a red fox
- ⭕ a big pot
- ⭕ a big ox
- ⭕ a can of wax

- ⭕ a red box
- ⭕ a box of mix
- ⭕ six hot mugs
- ⭕ six big logs
- ⭕ a red ax

6

91

It can sit in a den.

It can run in the sun.

It can hop on a log.

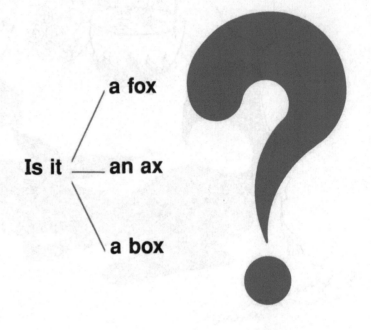

Is it
a fox
an ax
a box

It is big.

It can tug a big tub.

It can lug a big log.

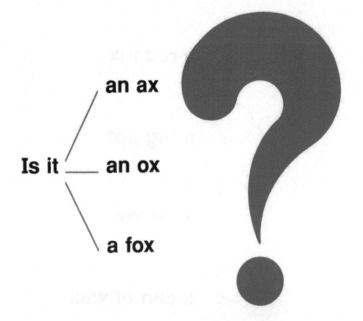

Is it
an ax
an ox
a fox

Is it in the Big Top?

	Yes	No
A man is in a net.	⊗	◯
A man is at the top.	◯	◯
A fox sits on a box.	◯	◯
A cub is on a tub.	◯	◯
The ax is in a log.	◯	◯
A can has wax in it.	◯	◯
A hat has lots of dots on it.	◯	◯

I am red.

My bed is in a den.

I am as big as a dog.

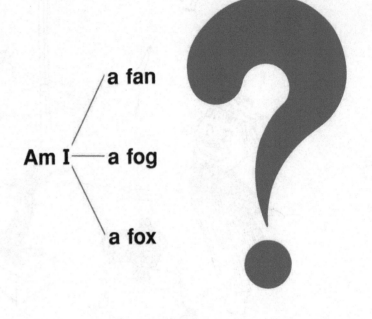

a fan

Am I — a fog

a fox

I got a big red box.

The box had a pet in it.

I am big and I am six.

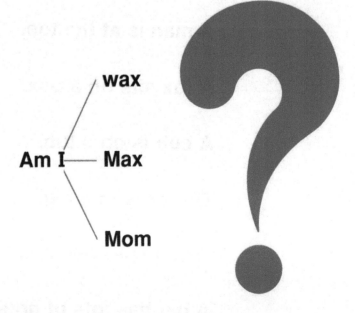

wax

Am I — Max

Mom